I call her Mummy, she calls me brave

Author Nicola Owen
Illustrated by Noor Alshalabi

For Dylan and Poppy, my inspiration,

my reason, my all.

Foreword

As a mum living with stage 4 breast cancer, it was important for me to create a resource that reflected the reality that some cancers will not be cured, however it felt equally important to acknowledge that thanks to research and incredible medical developments many stage 4 patients are able to live well for longer.

This story aims to introduce incurable cancer to young children and address their feelings and experiences as a parent goes through treatment.

While I now live with an incurable cancer of my own, I also lost my mum to cancer while I was in my teenage years, so this is a topic that I am passionate about for many reasons. I know all too well that desire to protect the people we love from the things that scare us, but I have learnt first-hand that honesty and inclusion helps build resilience and avoids leaving children feeling isolated, scared, and confused. The way in which we discuss this difficult topic with our children is of course unique and individual, which is why this story has been created to provide a starting point, a way to open the conversation, a building block to allow you to tailor the conversation with your child to suit your own individual circumstances.

Best wishes

Nicola

Just yesterday I grazed my knee, I fell off my bike and it started to bleed. Lucky for me my Mummy was on hand with a magical kiss, a warm hug, and a plaster just for me.

I cried a little, but Mummy says that is ok, only the truly brave are strong enough to show their pain and upset. Mummy said it's always best to share the way we feel, especially when we are sad or cross, we don't need to hide away.

But I think Mummy is the bravest, she shows us every day, there is always a reason to be grateful even on our hardest days.

My Mummy has a cancer and not the kind that goes away. Cancer is an illness that grows inside the body, harming any body part that gets in its way.

It takes a team of people to help her, doctors, nurses, therapists, and friends, but importantly its family that helps Mummy through each day.

My Daddy's always lots of fun and likes to teach me new things and my Grandad is the greatest, with big arms to give the best cuddles. My Aunty and My Uncle make the best babysitters when Mummy and Daddy are not around, and Nanny always helps us out in any way she can.

RED
GREEN

There are so many different medicines and hospital visits mummy must go to, to help keep the cancer at bay, tablets, injections, and lots of tests to make sure she is ok.

There's a special type of medicine called chemotherapy, it's a poison to the cancer, and fights hard to stop it growing, but this can cause lots of changes. Mummy might start to look different, sometimes she gets tired and sometimes feels poorly, she may even lose her hair.

I feel worried when she is too sore for a cuddle, our hugs are always the best, but I know I can count on my Grandad for a cuddle when Mummy just needs to rest.

Mummy likes nothing more than sharing in our fun, dancing round the living room, and playing all day long, but on the days when mummy is tired and does not want to play, or maybe she is feeling sad, and needs a little cry, I know that plenty of rest in her comfy bed will help her get through.

Mummy says that time is precious, a lesson for us all. She wants me to remember that cancer is no one's fault, some people are just chosen for no good reason at all.

Her battle will continue now for all the days to come, with endless hospital visits, but we can still have lots of fun. We will make the best of all our good days, with so many new adventures to explore, and share our difficult feelings when we are angry, hurt or upset, just like I did when I grazed my knee.

No matter where the path takes us in time to come, I know that I am always loved, and even when I am feeling worried or sad, I do not need to feel alone.

www.ingramcontent.com/pod-product-compliance
Ingram Content Group UK Ltd.
Pitfield, Milton Keynes, MK11 3LW, UK
UKHW051359110225
4527UKWH00093B/125

9 781838 418113